An experience of cliffs

Sensing of place. As a boy, I delighted in time spent alone on these cliffs. After a day amongst low-tide rock pools, I would, as the tide advanced, scramble up the cliff, to lie on its edge, my head cushioned by sea-pinks. Against my back, the bare rock held the warm memory of the sun. I remember, eyes closed, working through each sense in turn. The soft, low roar of surf against which gulls cried, so much part of this place that, until addressed, it remained unheard. Then, as now, there was the coconut smell of gorse or, lifting from the rocks, the tang of drying seaweed. My lips tasted of salt. A tickling insect moved through the hairs on my leg. The unconscious sum of that was 'a sensing of place'.

A sense of place. Later there developed a curiosity as to the form of rocks and the power of the sea. In retrospect, I like to imagine these were the seeds, which directed me towards geography. Eventually, as a lecturer in geomorphology at Oxford Brookes University, with a special interest in the evolution of coastal landscapes, I returned to this area regularly throughout my career.

Knowledge, derived from a range of disciplines, together with the much less structured pleasure of simply experiencing this coast, combined to provide what is best described as 'a sense of place'.

A sense of time. Perhaps of a different order is the satisfaction of being able to 'read the landscape', both physical and human. This includes an understanding of the way the landscape is always in a state of change on a variety of scales and at different speeds. To appreciate what has brought the landscape to its present condition we need a sense of time.

Exploring the coast. Many of those walking west on the coastal path from Westward Ho! are exhilarated by the spectacular scenery of cliffs and shore and have their curiosity aroused as to the origins and evolution of this dramatic coastal landscape. This booklet is for such people, written in the hope that it blends the satisfaction of knowledge with the enjoyment of experiencing this still-wild stretch of coast.

The plentiful illustrations are included, in part, so that even if you are only able to walk these cliffs in your imagination, then you can still enjoy th

Peter Keene   1st October 200

1

Structure of the book

walking directions

Yellow panels give directions to each of the viewpoints on the walk. These instructions can be used in conjunction with the map on the rear cover.

Commentary and observations

Blue banners flag text which is best described as a 'landscape companion' offering a straightforward but stimulating commentary and description of the local landscape which can be appreciated by both visitors and residents.

Layers of time

The landscape holds a memory of past events. These are revealed layer by layer. History, archaeology, geomorphology and geology all contribute to the resonance of this place. A little imagination allows us to travel in time, adding an extra dimension to the walk. The first layer, below, is a transient human veneer, one afternoon on the beach at Westward Ho! in 1984.

ⓘ Information and explanation

The green panels offer additional information for those who take pleasure in 'reading the landscape' in more detail. Although not essential for the casual enjoyment of the walk, this art of inquisitive interpretation in the field, adds interest to the way we explore the landscape. These panels also provide a more permanent source of reference for the themes which emerge.

The Cliffs of
Westward Ho!
a sense of time

Stretching our sense of time

The most immediate and readily understood changes in the landscape are those that have taken place on a time-scale of a few generations. We start the walk on a scale measured in a hundred years or so. As the walk progresses, the time-scale increases to include landscape changes over thousands, then millions of years, by which time our imagination and sense of time may be stretched to its limits.

Kipling Tors

Walking to Viewpoint A

From Seafield House, see the rear cover map, walk directly inland up a short track which ends after some 50 metres, at the foot of a hillside known as Kipling Tors, a National Trust property. From the base of the uncultivated hill-slope follow the path which climbs diagonally up the hillside to your left. After some 100 metres a path branches off to the right but continue on the main path for another 200 metres until you reach a staggered crossroads of paths. Turn right following the path which, after a brief climb, contours the hillside westwards. Pause at the wayside bench, or when you have a clear view out over the bay. We will call this viewpoint A.

100 years ago

A changing landscape

Our first step back in time is about a century. The artist's view on the hand-tinted postcard above is approximately that seen from this viewpoint (A) looking eastwards. The card is postmarked 23 August 1907. Printed text on the back of the card describes Westward Ho (with no !) of that time and reads:

"Westward Ho Born of speculative builders in the early fifties, and christened after Kingsley's famous story, Westward Ho has grown up out of nothing into a little but rather pretty scattering of villas among golf links. At the United Services College here, Rudyard Kipling was educated. Westward Ho is fifteen minutes' railway run from Bideford."

4

Now and Then

Clearly Westward Ho! has expanded dramatically since the postcard view of 1907, some would say, aesthetically, not for the better. However, some buildings in the postcard view can still be identified, in particular those clustered about what is today the slipway (V). You will not be able to pick out the large pink building. This was the Pebbleridge Hotel, the first hotel to open in Westward Ho! (1865) but this was demolished in 1993 to make way for bungalows (I). On the postcard, to the right of the hotel, Westbourne Terrace and Springfield Terrace can be identified.

Not visible on the postcard would have been the church (D) opened in 1870 and the grand 'Westward Ho! Hotel' (opened in 1865). This later became the 'Royal Hotel' and then the 'Golden Bay Hotel'. It was eventually knocked down to be replaced by a complex of apartments called Ocean Park (B).

Both then and now, across Northam Burrows we can see, just to the left of Staddon Hill (G), the riverside fishing village of Appledore.

In 1907, out of sight at the foot of Kipling Tors, then called Furze Hill, you might have heard a steam engine struggling up the slope out of Westward Ho! then to run along the cliff-top to Cornborough before turning inland - *"fifteen minutes' railway run from Bideford".*

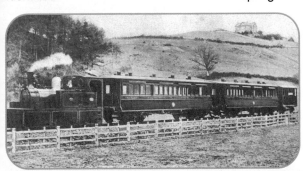

This postcard, postmarked September 20th 1904, shows the train puffing up the Kenwith Valley towards Cornborough.

1797 ▶

2003 ▶

A landscape bonus

In 1797, Thomas Girtin, an English watercolourist (1775-1802), visited Devon and Dorset. Whilst touring, he made a series of outdoor colour 'sketches' (including a well-known watercolour of Appledore from Instow). By his death in 1802, cataloguing was incomplete. The 1797 watercolour, above, was listed as Porlock Bay. Eventually, as part of the Paul Mellon Collection, the painting ended up at the 'Yale Center of British Art', Connecticut. Its true identity was only recognised recently, shortly before being exhibited in Tate Britain in 2002. We are thus provided with a newly revealed and unique view of this corner of Bideford Bay at the end of the eighteenth century.

Thomas Girtin stood above Appledore looking westwards from the flank of Staddon Hill (G), see pages 5 and 23. Comparison with a photograph taken from near the same location today (grid reference SS 459304) suggests that, although the watercolour might be regarded as a field sketch, its attention to detail and accuracy is remarkable.

Thomas Girtin's panorama

Girtin's panorama sweeps around Bideford Bay from Hartland Point on the far right, to the tower of Northam Church on the left-hand edge of the picture. In the centre is the wide, flat, coastal lowland of Northam Burrows. This plain of blue wandering streams, lakes and marshland is painted as it was, before straight ditches enhanced drainage to improve the grazing. In the left foreground, smoke rises from Diddywell whilst, nestling amongst trees to the right, is Watertown. On the horizon, to the right of a squat tower, a long dark horizontal shadow marks the steep slope of Kipling Tors where you are now standing (A).

The most dramatic difference between the landscape of Girtin's time and that which we view today is the complete absence of the village of Westward Ho! Charles Kingsley's novel "Westward Ho!" based in the locality, was published in 1855. The landscape seen by Charles Kingsley was essentially the same as that experienced by Girtin. In his novel, Kingsley describes how, about the estuary,

"the hills.... in softly-rounded knolls ... sink into the wide expanse of hazy flats, rich salt-marshes, and rolling sand hills, where Torridge joins her sister Taw, and both together flow quietly towards the broad surges of the bar; and the everlasting thunder of the long Atlantic swell."

Westward Ho! is born

Kingsley's landscape

The map above (Lt. Col. Mudge1809) is essentially the landscape in which Charles Kingsley wrote 'Westward Ho!'. The western corner of Northam Burrows was open farmland. A faint wisp of smoke on Girtin's sketch marks the site of what would become Westward Ho! and probably flags the farmstead of Venton (Ventown) or perhaps Youngaton (Youngington) - Y on the rear cover map, now the Village Inn. The area was sufficiently remote for Kingsley to have Amyas Leigh, the hero of the novel, walking down to the pebble ridge where he stripped and plunged naked into the surf.

A speculative venture

Westward Ho!, published in 1855, was an immediate success and *"awakened public interest in the romantic and beautiful coast of North Devon."* More significantly in 1856, the mainline railway from Exeter to Barnstaple was extended to Bideford. To some this seemed the moment to realise the potential of developing a fashionable seaside watering-place on the north coast to rival that of Torquay in South Devon. The 'Northam Burrows Hotel and Villas Company' was formed in 1863.

A scattering of villas

A 75-acre plot of land was purchased abutting the western end of Northam Burrows, upon which to develop a hotel, *"together with villas where families could reside for the season, or, if they preferred, purchase or rent the house for a term of years."*

What more appropriate name could there be for this new 'venture settlement' than Westward Ho! after the epic novel which first drew attention to the beauty of the district? The flag-ship hotel, The 'Westward Ho!', opened in 1865.

Kingsley, dismayed at the prospect of his beauty spot being overcome by a rash of speculative building unleashed by his successful novel, wrote mournfully to a Bideford friend,

"How goes on the Northam scheme for spoiling that beautiful place with hotels and villas? I suppose it must be – if there is a demand let it be supplied – but you will frighten away the seapies and defile the Pebble Ridge with chicken bones and sandwich scraps. The Universe is growing Cockney, and men like me must look out for a planet to live without fear of railways and villa projectors."

...the rest is history!

Victorian Westward Ho!

Kingsley College 1882-1885

30 years of coastal change

1870-1

Only seven years after the company was founded, Westward Ho! had already grown into what was described on the postcard as a *"little but rather pretty scattering of villas"*. The Westward Ho! Hotel (B) had already expanded to include a large annexe (C) described at the time as *"a capacious lodging house and cooking house, an adjunct for servants belonging to aristocratic visitors"*. It also had a bathing establishment (A) for ladies, with a large ball-room on the first floor. The bathing pool at the centre of the complex was supplied with sea water pumped by coal-fired steam engines (notice the chimney).

To complement an Upper Lodge, at the top of the hill, guarding the southern edge of the estate (see rear cover map), a Lower Lodge (E) was built at the north-eastern entrance to the estate. Westbourne Terrace (F) provided lodging houses within a 100 yard walk of the beach. The church (D) was added in 1870, and a post office established in Nelson Terrace (G).

1878-9

One thing that was clearly not appreciated by the developers at the time was the speed with which the sea was actively eroding the shore and pushing the Pebble Ridge landwards. Local reports as early as 1855 suggested that Northam Burrows was under threat and that *"the beach was so denuded as to threaten the safety of the Pebble Ridge itself."* Revd Gosset (1865).

Nevertheless, in 1875 optimistic developers built, within a stone's throw of the advancing sea, a grand Union Club (U) for the Royal North Devon Golf Club. The same building was hurriedly dismantled and moved inland less than 4 years later, by which time waves were throwing pebbles into the building. Soon Lower Lodge (E) was also dismantled and rebuilt 100 m inland (E_2).

1899-1900

By 1900 the sea had claimed another five houses at the lower end of Westbourne Terrace. The crest of the Pebble Ridge in 1870 (P) had, by 1900, been pushed 100 metres inland and the soft low cliffs of unconsolidated 'head' upon which much of lower Westward Ho! was built proved no more resistant than the Pebble Ridge to the advance of the sea. It was not until 1932 that a seawall and slipway (V) were built to protect the most vulnerable part of Westward Ho! Between 1861 and 1932 the shore was retreating at an average of 1.75 metres per year. The maximum loss of land between 1861 and 2004 has been 150 metres. It seems the physical coastal landscape has changed almost as quickly as the built environment. If you want to follow this topic further read "Westward Ho! Against the Sea" (see page 49).

6,000 years ago

Into pre-history

Some elements in the landscape change very rapidly, almost while we watch but most large-scale changes, even before we lose the human dimension, need to be viewed on a timescale of thousands of years rather than hundreds.

The next step in time takes us into the Stone Age. We know the climate was as warm if not warmer than today and that the natural vegetation of southern Britain was mainly mixed deciduous woodland but what was the environment and landscape like at Westward Ho! at that time?

Evidence from Westward Ho! beach provides an intriguing and detailed picture of exactly what life was like here 6,000 years ago.

Peat beds exposed

If the tide is out and the wide sandy beach is exposed, look towards the zone where the rocky shore and sandy beach together meet the sea. Here, on exceptionally low tides, you may see, peeping through the sand, a bank of heavily eroded dark peat, sandwiched in places between two layers of lighter, blue-grey clay.

The clay was laid down underwater in a sheltered estuarine environment but the layer of peat indicates that 6000 years ago this area was land. A layer of clay on top of the peat indicates that, some time later, estuary water returned. Six thousand years ago sea level was some 4 metres lower than today. The pebbleridge, if it existed then, would have been well to the seaward of the present low-water mark.

A sunken forest

Within the peat and rooting into the underlying clay, are preserved tree trunks and roots of oak, willow and hazel (see above), which confirm that 6,000 years ago this was a flat fresh-water land environment, a dense fen carr, with frequent damp, stagnant pools, containing frogs, bank voles and fresh-water shells.

When first described in 1863, some 40 trees were standing proud of the peat. Today the stumps have been all but eroded away by the sea, but on the peaty surface you can still see branches, twigs and hazel nuts, some so well-preserved that it is possible to see scratches (A) and teeth marks (B) of the small woodland animals, such as bank voles, which chewed at the nut.

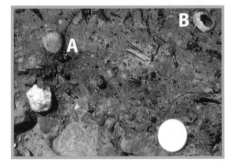

13

Middle Stone Age

Still more intriguing is evidence that these woodlands were occupied by the earliest recorded inhabitants of Westward Ho! These were Mesolithic hunter-gatherers who, among other things, speared fish, hunted game and cooked shellfish.

Kitchen Midden

Preserved between the peat and the underlying clay, a Stone Age rubbish tip (kitchen midden) was discovered. The bulk of the midden was composed of shell fragments of limpets, mussels, oysters and peppery furrow shells, presumably gathered from the seashore which can't have been that far away.

Charcoal and burnt animal bones suggest that these Mesolithic people were also hunters. Bones found nearby included those of red and roe deer, wild ox, hedgehog and domestic dog.

Flint tools found on-site included arrowheads, scrapers and knife blades. The abundance of flint shards indicates that these were made on the spot, probably by knapping small flint pebbles which are quite common on the modern beach.

Left: A Mesolithic, serrated carved bone harpoon from Westward Ho! beach on display at the 'Museum of Barnstaple and North Devon'
Below: Kitchen midden at Westward Ho! Mesolithic site.

A fish trap?

A line of wooden stakes hammered through the peat into the underlying clay have been variously interpreted as the remains of a Stone Age fish trap or perhaps the support for an ancient trackway across marshy ground.

The remnants of the stakes are now flush with the peat surface. On the photo they are marked by silver coins. The stakes, radiocarbon dated at 4,800 years old, were more recent than the kitchen midden and were probably constructed by Neolithic people.

Sometime after this episode, the peat beds were buried under blue clay as the area reverted once more to a shallow-water estuary environment.

An inner clay bank

This is not the end of the story. Wooden stakes and animal bones within a smaller area of peat exposed on the beach in the mid-tide zone (the inner clay bank) have been dated as 1,600 years old. It suggests that by Romano-British times the area was once again coastal fen.

These fluctuating conditions are typical of estuaries where migrating water channels and accumulating marshlands constantly displace each other.

A museum visit

With a little knowledge it is fascinating to walk out across the sands to inspect what remains of these sites. They are protected, so what survives of this 'outdoor museum' should not be disturbed.

However, not too far away, in the Square at the end of Barnstaple Bridge in the 'Museum of Barnstaple and North Devon', is a permanent display of some of the finds at the Westward Ho! site - well worth a visit.

A fossil landscape

It is not always appreciated that the shape of our landscape often owes more to changes linked to climates of the past rather than to processes which are active today. The hill upon which you are standing is no exception. A strong case can be made for this being a 'fossil' landscape, a relict inherited from a very different past.

As the temperature graph shows, only 18,000 years ago North Devon was in the middle of an ice age, a glacial period which saw much of Britain buried beneath its own ice sheet, in places almost 2 km thick.

Ice-sheet view

Standing at viewpoint A at that time, you probably would still have recognised Kipling Tors, for North Devon was not buried by an ice-sheet, although a tongue of the Welsh ice-sheet did reach south as far as the Gower Peninsula, only 35 miles (56 km) from here and this would have been visible, just to the left of Baggy Point. On a clear day you can see Worms Head from Kipling Tors, again, just to the left of Baggy Point.

Where was the sea?

Probably the really startling difference in the view would have been the absence of the sea. Imagine the floor of Bideford Bay as a treeless plain of moss and bog. This tundra-like wilderness stretched as far as the eye could see, eventually to terminate

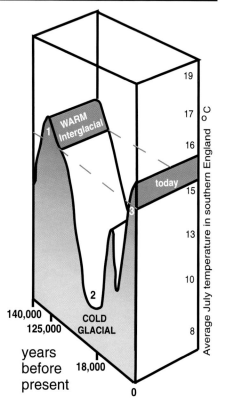

among the braided outwash spreads of gravel issuing from the snout of the Welsh ice-sheet.

The absence of the sea from the Bristol Channel was intimately linked to the presence of vast continental ice sheets including the one which, at that time, covered much of the British Isles. Why was the sea level so low?

(i) Information panels on pages 17 to 19 answer this question and offer more details about what was happening on Kipling Tors during the last Ice Age.

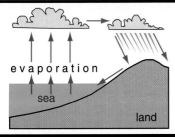

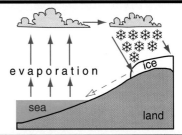

The water cycle in balance — *The water cycle interrupted*

Upsetting the water cycle

One dramatic effect of stages of intense cold (ice ages) is the change brought about to world sea level. Sea levels only remain relatively stable as long as the water cycle is uninterrupted, see above. Under very cold conditions some winter snowfall will fail to melt in the following summer and instead pack down to form glacier ice, thickening year by year to create thick ice sheets. This upsets the water cycle, because insufficient water returns to the sea to balance losses due to evaporation. Such cold stages are therefore associated with low world sea levels.

Low sea levels

The most recent cold stage reached its most severe about 18,000 years ago. North Devon was not covered by an ice sheet at this time but the presence of vast continental ice sheets elsewhere is linked to a world-wide fall in sea level of some 120 metres. However, locally these ice-sheets were sufficiently thick and heavy to depress the earth's crust and so, in places like North Devon, peripheral to the Welsh ice-sheet, the actual local fall in sea level experienced has been difficult to determine.

Rising sea levels

After the last cold stage, the world warmed again, and most of the great continental ice caps gradually melted. The sea came flooding back into Bideford Bay. By 6,000 years ago, when the Mesolithic hunter-gatherers lived here, sea level was only four metres lower than today. In the last 3,000 years sea level has only risen by a couple of metres and the water cycle was considered as being in rough balance.

The greenhouse effect

However, almost certainly related to industrialisation and the greenhouse effect, the last remaining continental ice sheets are now melting faster than fresh ice can accumulate through snowfall and so sea levels are again rising.

Locally this sea level rise threatens coastal lowlands such as Northam Burrows and Braunton Burrows as well as the river frontages of tide-water towns such as Bideford, Instow and Appledore. Here, river defences have already been enhanced in anticipation of rising sea level and increasing climatic instability.

Arctic wastes

During the coldest stage of the most recent ice age (18,000 years ago) North Devon was not covered by an ice sheet but the proximity of the Welsh ice-sheet only 35 miles to the north meant that Kipling Tors experienced an arctic-like periglacial climate. The slope you are standing on (A) would have supported only a thin covering of moss and lichens clinging to rock and slope debris.

Creating a straight slope

In periglacial conditions water, penetrating rock joints, repeatedly froze and thawed, fragmenting the rock surface, creating a layer of broken angular stones and smaller debris on the surface. As the layer of debris grew thicker, it began to protect the buried rock from the most violent effects of freezing and thawing. However, any remaining solid rock, projecting through this hillside mantle of fragments, would still be susceptible to the effects of mechanical weathering (frost action), certainly more so than rock protected beneath the mantle of waste debris. In this way irregularities would be progressively removed and a regular (straight) rock slope would develop, buried beneath a superficial layer of broken rubble.

Relicts of the ice age

The creation of these straight slopes under periglacial conditions is very common but what is more remarkable is how many can still be recognised today, after thousands of years of the warmer climate which followed the ice age.

Kipling Tors is a good example of one of these relict slopes. The slope angle here is between 29° and 32°. This angle represents the limiting angle of stability of the debris mantle, which in turn is related to the size and angularity of the debris and the amount of water it contains.

These periglacial slopes have survived because in the warmer climate of today, much of the weathering is chemical. Material is dissolved in ground water and removed in solution without any apparent change in the appearance of the hillside. So, there is a strong case for suggesting that you are really standing on a fossil slope not much altered since the last ice age.

If you are not yet convinced that the hillside you are standing on is a rectilinear rock slope covered with a thin layer of debris, then look at the photo, right. This Kipling Tors quarry-side can be seen in more detail when you reach viewpoint C.

A pasty mess

The mean annual air temperature here 18,000 years ago was possibly 15°C colder than today and the ground was deep-frozen (permafrost). In summer the sun would melt winter surface snowfall and warm air would start to penetrate the ground, melting any ice in the ground near the surface, perhaps to a depth of two metres.

However, this melt-water could not percolate into the deeper, still-frozen layer beneath, which formed an impermeable barrier so the upper unfrozen ground was soon saturated with water, creating a pasty mess of water, fine debris and angular stones.

A hillside on the move

In summer, this lubricated mass would slowly sludge down the slope under the force of gravity, a few centimetres each year until, on the gentler slope at the foot of the hill, it would eventually come to a halt. Accumulating over the years, this deposit, known as 'head', would cover the ground in a thick apron of angular frost-shattered stones within a mass of finer debris.

This is why, despite many, many years of frost action during the cold stage, so little broken angular debris is found on the hillside itself. It all slid down the hill to collect at the bottom. Perhaps you can identify the area where it has collected on the photograph below?

125,000 years ago

A warm stage

The next jump back in time is to a warm stage 125,000 years ago. The picture, right, give or take the odd white Art Deco hotel, could be the view from Kipling Tors 125,000 years ago. The temperature chart, page 16, confirms that England, at that time, was experiencing a warm stage (an interglacial) with temperatures similar to, or a little warmer, than today. During warm stages, continental ice-sheets were relatively small and therefore world sea levels were high, similar to but a little higher than today's.

Fossil sea cliffs

At the peak of this high sea-level stage (called the Ipswichian), waves cut fresh-faced, steep, sea cliffs around the flanks of Bideford Bay at about eight metres higher than today's sea level. Kipling Tors, although subsequently weathered and degraded was, then, part of this line of sea-cliffs fringing Bideford Bay.

Can you trace, by eye, the line of former cliffs eastwards from Kipling Tors, passing behind Northam Burrows, to Appledore and Instow? The line of the former cliff-line can be picked up again near Braunton, behind Braunton Burrows, joining the modern sea-cliffs close to the white hotel at Saunton, seen across the bay. The path of the old cliff-line is clearly marked on page 23.

Landscape evolution

We now have enough information to reconstruct a sequence of events which shaped Kipling Tors and the cliffs of Westward Ho! over the last

125,000 years. On this timescale most of the landscape evolution is related to the major climatic changes which occurred as the district slipped in and out of an ice age.

The evolution of the local cliffs is summarised in the illustration on the next page. The model can be used to help explain the appearance of much of the coastal cliffs of southwest Britain.

The Evolution of the Cliffs of Westward Ho!

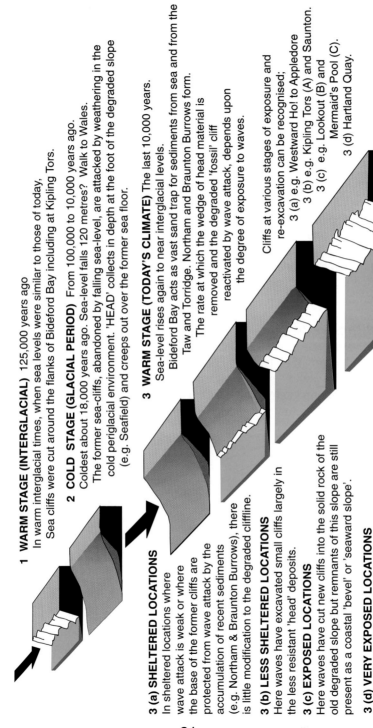

1 WARM STAGE (INTERGLACIAL) 125,000 years ago
In warm interglacial times, when sea levels were similar to those of today,
Sea cliffs were cut around the flanks of Bideford Bay including at Kipling Tors.

2 COLD STAGE (GLACIAL PERIOD) From 100,000 to 10,000 years ago.
Coldest about 18,000 years ago. Sea-level falls 120 metres? Walk to Wales.
The former sea-cliffs, abandoned by falling sea-level, are attacked by weathering in the
cold periglacial environment. 'HEAD' collects in depth at the foot of the degraded slope
(e.g. Seafield) and creeps out over the former sea floor.

3 WARM STAGE (TODAY'S CLIMATE) The last 10,000 years.
Sea-level rises again to near interglacial levels.
Bideford Bay acts as vast sand trap for sediments from sea and from the
Taw and Torridge. Northam and Braunton Burrows form.
The rate at which the wedge of head material is
removed and the degraded 'fossil' cliff
reactivated by wave attack, depends upon
the degree of exposure to waves.

Cliffs at various stages of exposure and
re-excavation can be recognised;
3 (a) e.g. Westward Ho! to Appledore
3 (b) e.g. Kipling Tors (A) and Saunton.
3 (c) e.g. Lookout (B) and
Mermaid's Pool (C).
3 (d) Hartland Quay.

3 (a) SHELTERED LOCATIONS
In sheltered locations where
wave attack is weak or where
the base of the former cliffs are
protected from wave attack by the
accumulation of recent sediments
(e.g. Northam & Braunton Burrows), there
is little modification to the degraded cliffline.

3 (b) LESS SHELTERED LOCATIONS
Here waves have excavated small cliffs largely in
the less resistant 'head' deposits.

3 (c) EXPOSED LOCATIONS
Here waves have cut new cliffs into the solid rock of the
old degraded slope but remnants of this slope are still
present as a coastal 'bevel' or 'seaward slope'.

3 (d) VERY EXPOSED LOCATIONS
In very exposed locations with a high wave-energy environment such as
the Hartland coast, cliff cutting has been very active and has completely
removed the periglacial 'seaward slope'.

21

Temperature cycles

The explanation given on the previous pages for the evolution of the local coastal landscape over the last 125,000 years seems to fit what we see on the ground very well but this explanation needs qualifying.

If the temperature chart shown on page 16 is extended back into the more distant past (see below) it is clear that the sequence of a warm stage (interglacial) followed by a cold stage (ice age) is a cycle that has re-occurred many times.

Shorelines revisited

At least eight ice ages have been recognised over the last 740,000 years. These cold stages were separated by warm interglacial stages. Sea-levels fluctuated, roughly following the temperature curves. In the warm interglacials, sea-levels rose, often revisiting and modifying the same shoreline several times. The landforms we see may therefore be the combined sum of a number of such episodes.

Fluctuating ice sheets

Ice caps grew during cold stages but there is no evidence of an ice-sheet ever engulfing Devon. However 450,000 years ago an ice-sheet did advanced from Wales across the dry Bristol Channel and entered Bideford Bay. Glacial deposits at Fremington and Lake (Barnstaple) suggest that at this time the ice front had at least blocked the lower course of the River Taw. The view north from here would have been dominated by this vast ice-sheet, its steep flanks towering above you.

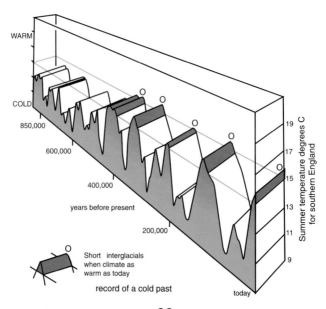

WARM

COLD

850,000

600,000

years before present

400,000

200,000

Summer temperature degrees C for southern England

19

17

15

13

11

9

today

O Short interglacials when climate as warm as today

record of a cold past

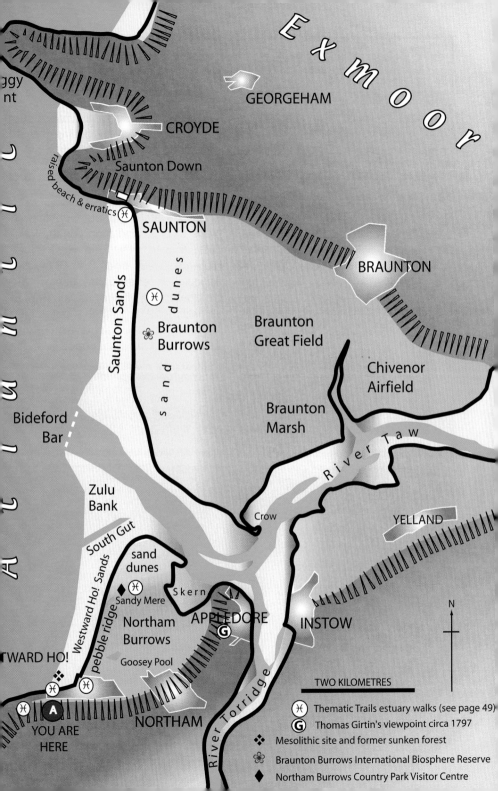

EXMOOR

GEORGEHAM

CROYDE

Saunton Down

raised beach & erratics

SAUNTON

BRAUNTON

Saunton Sands

sand dunes

Braunton Burrows

Braunton Great Field

Chivenor Airfield

Bideford Bar

Braunton Marsh

River Taw

Zulu Bank

South Gut

Crow

YELLAND

sand dunes

Westward Ho! Sands

pebble ridge

Sandy Mere

Skern

APPLEDORE

INSTOW

Northam Burrows

G

Goosey Pool

WARD HO!

NORTHAM

River Torridge

A

YOU ARE HERE

N

TWO KILOMETRES

⊕ Thematic Trails estuary walks (see page 49)

Ⓖ Thomas Girtin's viewpoint circa 1797

❖ Mesolithic site and former sunken forest

✿ Braunton Burrows International Biosphere Reserve

◆ Northam Burrows Country Park Visitor Centre

The coastguard look-out

Walking to viewpoint B

From viewpoint A, walk westward, contouring Kipling Tors, until after about 600 metres you meet a path climbing diagonally up the hillside from your right. Turn left, up this path. After about 50 metres there is an abandoned look-out. This is viewpoint B, seen as a white spot in the centre of this photo.

History of the look-out

In December 1909 a steamer, the 'Thistlemoor', sank off Clovelly with the loss of 20 lives. Local feelings ran high as this was considered, "a preventable loss of life", due to the lack of a good coast watch system. Within the month, after a meeting in Bideford, volunteers launched the 'North Devon Association for the Efficient Watching of our Coasts' with plans to build and man coastal look-outs of which this, the Rock Nose look-out was one. In 1911 the Association offered the use of the look-out to the official coastguards. In January 1912, "their objectives having been achieved", the Association was disbanded.

A room with a view

The balcony gives a fine view of Bideford Bay from Hartland Point in the west to Baggy Point in the north-east. With winds constantly driving Atlantic waves into the bay, it is easy to see how Bideford Bay became a vast trap for coastal sediments which were pushed to the head of the bay forming Northam and Braunton Burrows. Where the sediment-laden Rivers Taw and Torridge combine to enter the sea, sand-bank shallows form a bar over which waves can be seen breaking at most stages of the tide. In the middle of the bay some 19 miles from here is the granite slab of Lundy (Norse for puffin island). On a summer's evening this is a good place from which to watch the sun sink silently into the sea.

Turning the corner

At Kipling Tors, viewpoint A, the coastal cliffs face north and are relatively sheltered from Atlantic storm waves. The sea has not significantly eroded the degraded rock slope of the ancient interglacial cliff. This is a 3b situation (see page 21).

The distance between A and B is only 650 metres but the coastline has swung around to face the north-west. This is a more exposed shore and gets the full blast of Atlantic storms. As a result the cliffs here are significantly more eroded. This is a 3c situation! There is nothing but sea on a line from here to Boston, Massachusetts. The relative exposure of the two sites can be appreciated on the coastal photograph (circa 1984) on the previous page.

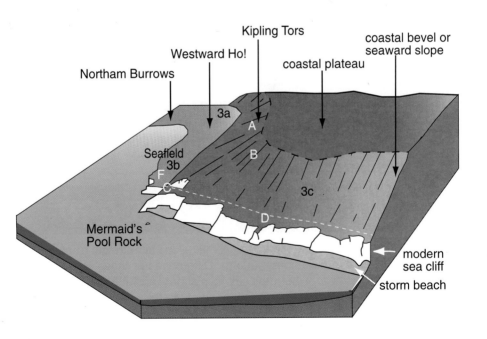

Bideford Bay (Jo Keene) circa 1960

Mermaid's Pool overlook

Walking to viewpoint C

From viewpoint B, retrace your steps for 50 metres and then continue diagonally down the hill by the roughly-stepped path until you reach the foot of the Tors. Here you will meet a stone-based track coming out from Westward Ho! Turn left to follow this track westwards. After a few metres the track opens out to reveal, on the left, two old cliff-top quarries. This is viewpoint C.

DO NOT APPROACH THE UNSTABLE CLIFF EDGE

The view is spectacular but as you may see from the cracks running along the cliff edge, landslips and cliff failures are common and the tufty cliff-edge grass is often unsupported from beneath.

300 million years ago

A t low tide the ancient rocks which make up this stretch of coast are exposed across the shore platform. Differences in these rocks help to control the shape of both the shore platform and the local cliffs. The greatest leap back in time we shall attempt is to picture this scene in Carboniferous times when the rocks we see today were first formed.

Local geologist **CHRIS CORNFORD** picks up the story.

26

Landscape on the grandest scale

"Looking out to sea one can imagine the landscape of 300 million years ago. Today we can see (on a clear day) the fussy line of the South Wales coastline, but imagine this as a vast river delta, the river being one of many draining a large landmass which lay to the north and ran roughly from Poland to Pennsylvania (at this time the Atlantic does not exist).

On this distant flat delta plain, dense tropical fern forests grow, with dead 'trees' accumulating to eventually form the coal seams of modern South Wales. Looking to the south, towards Cornwall, we would see mountains and possibly feel the rumble of earthquakes as the two major tectonic plates collided.

We stand on the northerly plate (Eurussia). To the south lay the southerly plate (Gondwana) comprising present day Spain, Africa, South America, Australia and Antarctica. Being squeezed between these two plates was the Rheic Ocean.

The soft sediments deposited on this ocean floor were buried, consolidated, crumpled and broken into a broad band of mountainous terrain called the 'Variscan' Mountains. Once, these mountains were probably similar in size and height to the Alps but today all we can see of these former ranges are the folded and faulted (fractured) layers of rocks from deep within the mountain chain, now exposed beneath our feet."

Northern Continent (Eurussia)

Equator

Rheic Ocean

WESTWARD HO

Southern Continent (Gondwana)

A more local prospect

"But what was it like at the actual location of Westward Ho! some 300 million years ago? We are standing in the middle of a fresh-water lake – locally termed Lake Bude – which lies between the swamps of the South Wales area and the mountains of Cornwall to the south. A small river flows out of the mountains and into the muddy waters of the lake. Clouds are gathering over the mountains and a smudge of grey in the distance indicates a curtain of rain. The small river swells to a flood, carrying sand and mud out into the basin, the flood currents scouring channels deep into the mud floor of the lake."

Chris Cornford (300 mybp).

Resulting from such floods, sheets of fine mud deposits alternating with coarser beds of sands were laid down in repeated cycles, either

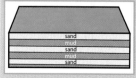

because the depth of water kept changing or because the water channels of the delta periodically altered their course.

These sediments were subsequently deeply buried and compressed

to produce folds, and c r a c k e d (fractured) to p r o d u c e faults. Here the mudstones and sandstones are steeply folded.

To appreciate the size and nature of these structures we need to be able to see a great slice across the rocks, a section exposing the folds and faults. As luck would have it, we have one which was prepared earlier! Standing well back from the cliff edge, look down onto the foreshore. It is clear that the wide shore platform cut

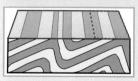

by the sea (a w a v e - c u t p l a t f o r m) provides a near-perfect horizontal cross-section through the local folds and faults. The red-dotted zone on the diagram roughly corresponds to the area covered by the photo opposite. The photo also provides a convenient substitute for the real thing if it is high tide.

At high tide this wave-cut platform is under water, although the highest outcrop of rock, just beyond Mermaid's Pool, usually stands above the waves. Can you identify this 'stack' at high tide in the photograph on page 24?

The beds of sandstone and mudstone in the Mermaid's Pool area were so heavily folded that here the beds are now almost vertical. Imagine each bed of sediment being one page of this booklet. Shut the book and tilt it on end. The view of the page-ends is similar to your view of the rock beds on the shore.

Which are the sandstones?

The massive sandstone beds are relatively resistant to erosion and generally stand out as prominent ridges of paler rock. The sandstones look pale grey partly because of the nature of the rock but also, being upstanding and exposed they are not colonised by the dark seaweeds.

Which are the mudstones?

The less resistant thinly bedded mudstones occupy the less prominent parts of the shore platform and are partly masked by the thick dark fronds of bladder-wrack seaweeds. The softer more readily eroded mudstones also tend to form the indentations or bays within the shore platform.

BIDEFORD BAY
f f
sandstone
mudstone
mudstone
Mermaid's
Pool
mudstone   sandstone   mudstone

ⓘ Faults, fractures and gullies

The rapid release of built-up pressure (stress) within the earth's crust produces fractures (faults), or fracture zones which allow the movement of the rock sequence on one side of the fracture relative to the other.

The fracture zones, which flag the faultlines f - f on this rocky shore, are quite easy to pick out because they are zones of weakness, avenues which can be exploited by the sea to erode long, steep-sided gullies running straight across the rocks.

Follow the ridge of pale sandstone which runs seawards from Mermaid's Pool and see how, each time the sandstone beds cross a fault-line (indicated by a gully), the beds have been displaced by movement along the fault.

29

The beds of sandstones and mudstones recognised on the shore platform continue into the cliff beneath us and are exposed as solid rock in the face of the disused quarry behind.

Can you distinguish mudstone from sandstone in the quarry face? Superficially they may look rather similar - a rusty brown. This is because water passing through the many joints within the 'solid' rock has, over time, stained the rocks with iron, the rusty brown colour. Lichens have also tended to discolour any rock surfaces exposed to light and water for long enough.

However, if you like a little challenge before moving to the next site then, by using the table below you should be able to work out which is which. The piles of fragmented rock at the foot of the quarry face, a scree, provide convenient samples which can be handled with safety.

ROCK TYPE	COLOUR	HARDNESS	GRAIN SIZE	COMMENT
1 SANDSTONE (from sand)	Light grey or rusty brown	Very hard and brittle	Coarse, (rough to touch)	Massive, thick beds
2 MUDSTONE (from mud)	Dark grey-black	Softer, scrapes with knife	Fine (smooth to touch)	Thinner, layered

Which way next?

If you opt for the shorter loop, then this is the point where you can swing back towards Seafield and Westward Ho! To pick up the commentary for the return walk via viewpoint F, turn to page 44.

Alternatively, continue westwards by immediately entering a cutting of the old cliff-top railway. This is also the route of the long-distance Coast Path. Pause when you have a good view ahead down the length of the cutting.

We continue the theme of a landscape in a constant state of change.
" In this World only change is permanent."

The railway cutting.

Coastal path and railway

The Bideford to Westward Ho! railway, opened in 1901. The cliff-top section of the railway, between here and Cornborough offered spectacular views out into the bay and was popular with holidaymakers. In 1905 the railway carried 130,000 passengers and in 1908 was extended to Appledore. Yet the railway never paid its way and when in 1917 the engines were commandeered for use at the front in France, the directors must have heaved a sigh of relief. The railway was never reopened after the war. However, until comparatively recently, on a frosty morning walk, a ghostly track (above) could still be seen in the cutting beyond the quarry.

Now walk down the track with ecologist **JANET KEENE** who looks at the cutting with the passage of time in mind.

The cutting, a passage of time

"The railway cutting was dug just over 100 years ago. The excavations exposed sandstones and mudstones which would initially have been bare, devoid of plant life or soil. All the abundant plant life you see today has arrived sometime over the past 100 years. This gradual cumulative colonisation by plants is called succession.

First colonisers

Initially nothing grows on the bare rock and some patches of scree are still too mobile to allow colonisation. However, if you look towards places where there are still steep rock faces, you will see that they are not completely bare. Notice the patches of grey lichens. These are the first colonisers and they are well-adapted to life on bare rock. They are composed of a sponge-like fungus which can absorb any rain water trickling down the rock face. Inside, protected by the fungus, are minute algae which can make sugars by photosynthesis. The spongy fungus, supplies the algae with water and salts and in return receives food so both benefit by the association.

Algae on their own can only grow where it is damp. Where water trickles down the rock face there are brilliant green algae. In hollows, where a rudimentary soil is beginning to collect, note the bright green mosses.

Soil accumulation

Gradually as soil accumulates, plants and consequently animals, can become established. Soil forms in several ways. Some comes from debris which has fallen down the cliff from above, some is by weathering of the rock and also from the action of chemicals secreted by lichens onto the rock which start to break it down. When the lichens die they add organic matter to the developing soil.

As the soil collects, flowering plants, which have roots, can germinate and grow. Fleshy stonecrop can survive both drought, which is a problem on these steep slopes with very thin-soils, and the salt spray blown in from the sea.

A climax community?

In the more sheltered parts of the cutting, ivy climbs the rock face and sweet-scented honeysuckle blooms

in summer but it is probable that, with the unforgiving conditions experienced on these exposed cliffs, this site has reached its climax community. That is, the largest and most complex set of organisms that the habitat can support.

Cliff-top prospect

At the end of the cutting, cross the stile and walk down the springy grass slope on your right to where you can sit in comfort and safety with a cliff-top panorama. This is viewpoint D.

This cliff-top sweep hosts an amazing variety of wild plants. It makes a colourful scene in summer. All the flowers in this booklet were photographed on one day in May 2004. What decides what will grow here?

ⓘ What decides what will grow here?

Thin soils

On the cliff-tops, a shallow soil has developed. Being derived from the underlying sandstones and mudstones, these soils are acidic. All along the North Devon coast are the remains of lime kilns where limestone from South Wales was roasted to make quicklime which was used for mortar in buildings and also to lime the acidic farmland soils.

Although vegetation here may have been modified by grazing and occasional fires, it is unlikely that this cliff-top was ever limed or cultivated. Wild plants proliferate, at least those which tolerate acidic soils, salt and exposure. Here colonisation and succession has taken place over millennia.

Exposure to wind and salt

Cliff-top colonists need to be able to tolerate drought by evaporation, caused by strong winds and sun. They are also exposed to salt spray in the wind and therefore need to be tolerant to concentrations of sea salt in the soil which would be fatal to many other plants. Plants which can tolerate salt are called halophytes. They can thrive in these places, where they are not in competition with more vigorous inland plants.

In more sheltered hollows there are colourful displays of spring flowers, such as primroses and violets, followed in May by bluebells especially among the bracken on Kipling Tors. In more exposed locations salt-tolerant (halophytic) plants are established, including thrift, sea campion, buck's-horn plantain and Danish scurvygrass.

ⓘ Salt & wind tolerant cliff-top plants

Thrift or Sea pink

(*Armeria maritima*) The cliff face and cliff-tops are dotted with the dense cushions of thrift or sea pink. The narrow leaves are tightly packed and

fleshy and anchored by very long, tough, branching roots. The roundish heads of pink flowers are in bloom from April to October. Thrift has a moderate to high tolerance of salinity thanks to salt glands which can excrete excess salt.

Sea campion (*Silene maritima*)

The white-flowered sea campion is often found among the sea pinks. Like thrift, its low cushion-like mat enables it to survive the strong onshore winds of winter storms.

Gorse (Ulex spp.)

Gorse grows on the cliff-top, in the cutting and over much of the Tors. In the absence of grazing and woodland trees, gorse can form a dense scrub. It is an evergreen perennial.

Often plants which thrive on cliff-tops are xerophytic, meaning that they can survive dry conditions. Typically these plants have leaves with a small surface area, for example the spine-like leaves of gorse. This reduces water lost by evapo-transpiration from the leaves, which is a great threat in an area such as this, that is exposed to strong winds for much of the year. To make up for this loss of leaf surface area, the gorse stems are green and also carry out photosynthesis but they have fewer stomata (pores for gas-exchange) and a thick cuticle to cut down water loss.

As with other plants of the pea family, gorse has nodules on its roots with nitrogen-fixing bacteria. In addition it has mycorrhizal associations with soil fungi which also increase its supply of essential nutrients.

The golden gorse flowers, with their scent of coconut, colour the cliffs for much of the year; hence the saying,

"When gorse is not in flower, kissing's not in season."

Common Dodder
(*Cuscuta epithymum*)

If you look at the gorse plants you may see a reddish web growing over some of them. This is dodder, a member of the Convolvulus or bindweed family and, like its relatives, it is a slender climbing plant. However, unlike other bindweeds, dodder is a parasite which lives on the gorse. Look out for its red tendrils twined around the gorse growing in the shelter of the railway cuttings.

In the spring the seed germinates and produces a root. Once dodder makes contact with gorse, it obtains water and minerals by penetrating the host plant. Once contact has been established the dodder root dies. The parasite's food also comes from its host. It no longer carries out photosynthesis and its leaves are reduced to scales. Without chlorophyll the stem is red. From July to September there are clusters of pale pink bell-shaped flowers at intervals along the stem.

35

Bracken *(Pteridium aquilinum)*

Bracken is a robust perennial fern which grows well on these cliff-tops as it thrives in a moderately acidic well-drained soil. However, it also grows best where humidity is high, yet appears to be doing well on the drier, wind-exposed slopes. In fact bracken has an extensive system of deep underground stems (rhizomes). This means that a plant which has established itself in a wet valley floor can creep up the sides of the valley, to areas that are dry and exposed, but can still obtain adequate water from the older part of the plant in the valley floor.

Like gorse, bracken too has mycorrhizal associations with soil fungi which increase its supply of nutrients in this thin soil. The above-ground part of the plant dies back in autumn which prevents excessive water loss in the fierce winter gales. It is also protected from predators as its fronds contain toxic chemicals.

The area of bracken seems to be expanding. In the past farmers deliberately set fire to parts of the Tors (swaling) to get rid of the gorse and bracken to improve grazing. The deep bracken rhizomes and the bluebells' underground bulbs allow them to survive these fires.

Rock Samphire
(Crithmum maritimum)

Many salt-tolerant plants like samphire have fleshy or succulent leaves which can store moisture at times of drought. Samphire is confined to rocky cliffs where its long roots enable it to penetrate cracks. Fully exposed to wind and salt, these plants may even be covered in salt crystals from dried spray.

Samphire is sometimes still collected and boiled with vinegar and spices to make a pickle. Climbing the cliffs was always a dangerous job. In King Lear, Edgar describes the cliffs near Dover:

"...half-way down hangs one that gathers samphire, dreadful trade! Methinks he seems no bigger than his head."

Turning towards the sea you may take pleasure in watching birds diving for fish. Gulls glide by making use of the cliff-face updraught. Black-and-white oyster-catchers search the intertidal rock platform for shellfish and juicy rock pool inhabitants. Cormorants, wings outstretched, perch on isolated rocks rising from the waves. A good cliff-top prospect."

Janet Keene (2004)

Some more cliff-top plants

Cornborough Cliffs

Walking to viewpoint E

Returning to the old railway, continue west through two small cuttings until, after some 700 metres, the track swings inland on a curved embankment towards the Kenwith Valley and Bideford. The coastal path veers right and immediately a fine view of the coast westwards unfolds. Pause. This is viewpoint E. Painting by Paul Lewin of Abbotsham.

The Cornborough shore

Where the wide Cornborough valley meets the sea (left-hand edge of the photo above), the cliffs are absent. A former lime kiln on this site conjures up images of Victorian two-masted sailing ships (ketches) struggling in through the surf near high tide, to run aground on the grey pebbles. Between the tides, donkeys hauled the limestone to the strand-side kiln. On the next tide the sailing boat would somehow have to burst out through the breakers to return to South Wales for the next load.

If, at some time you decide to walk further, you will find, at Green Cliff, Buck's Mills and Clovelly, some much better preserved ruined kilns linked to this once thriving local coastal industry. Apart from grazing, Cornborough valley was also once a race-course and later a rifle range. The old rifle butts are still visible.

Beyond Cornborough

At Cornborough it is pleasant to picnic on the springy coarse grass or to sit on the polished grey pebbles of the storm beach. If the tide is low enough, the rock pools of the shore platform invite exploration.

Beyond Cornborough the coastal path leads over Abbotsham Cliff (see page 42) and Green Cliff, passing an old lime kiln before climbing the great dark hog's back of Cockington (see page 37). Beyond Cockington, the sandy beach at Portledge and Peppercombe is backed by red sandstone cliffs, a splash of colour amidst the grey rocks of this coast.

The coastal path from Westward Ho! to Bucks Mills and Clovelly makes a comfortable day's walk providing you have arranged return transport. From Westward Ho! to Clovelly by coastal path is about 11 miles (17.5 km).

ⓘ How is this rocky shore formed?

Seen at low tide, the shore platform (or wave-cut platform) fringes the coast in both directions as far as the eye can see. It is 300 metres wide in places, a gently-sloping shelf cut into the land close to sea-level. The seaward edge of the shore platform is an indicator of where the cliff-line once stood (see section below).

Undermining the cliff-foot

At high tide the sea comes into direct contact with the cliff-foot. Storm waves smash pebbles against the cliff and also compress air trapped in rock cracks. As a wave falls back, the compressed air expands with explosive decompression which can blast blocks of rock from the cliff-face. Thus the cliff is undermined and eventually collapses. As long as fallen rocks can be swept away by waves this process can be repeated many times.

The shore platform survives

The eroded cliff creates new shore platform and so the total width of the platform will increase. But why is the rocky shore platform not destroyed by these same waves?

Because the energy of the waves penetrates to no great water depth and the waves are only adequately armed with stone debris at the cliff-foot, the shore platform can be regarded as the level below which the waves, at high tide, are comparatively ineffective as agents of erosion.

What about a timescale?

We know (page 17) that sea level has been more or less the same for the last 3,000 years. If the shore platform is 300 metres wide, an average rate of cliff retreat of 10 cm per year could be suggested. However, most earth scientists think this figure is far too high for a hard-rock coast so what else might be involved? The commentary and graph on page 22 show that fluctuating sea levels have revisited this shoreline many times in the past so that landforms such as the shore platform, and indeed the cliffs themselves, may well be composite features, the result of several high sea-level episodes of wave attack.

The retreating cliffs

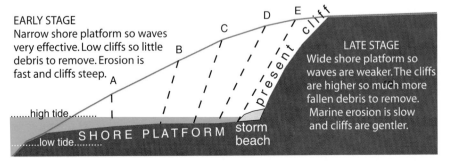

EARLY STAGE
Narrow shore platform so waves very effective. Low cliffs so little debris to remove. Erosion is fast and cliffs steep.

LATE STAGE
Wide shore platform so waves are weaker. The cliffs are higher so much more fallen debris to remove. Marine erosion is slow and cliffs are gentler.

present cliff

A B C D E

........high tide.........
........low tide.........   SHORE PLATFORM   storm beach

Landslides and aprons

Waves undermining the cliff precipitate landslides of rock debris which collects at the cliff-foot. This apron of mudstone fragments and sandstone blocks protects the cliff from further wave attack until it is dispersed.

Mudstone fragments

Mudstone fragments are relatively soft and weak and are soon broken down by waves into mud or silt. These particles are so fine that the waves soon lift them into suspension and they drift out to sea, eventually settling on the sea-floor to prepare the next generation of rocks. Mudstone fragments are not common on the beach except as part of newly arrived rock-falls.

Sandstone blocks

The more massive sandstone beds often fail along iron-stained joints and fall to the beach as large angular orange-brown blocks. Tumbled by the waves, these blocks are rounded and polished until they become the grey pebbles so familiar on this shore.

The storm beach

In shallow water, coarse sediments, including pebbles, are pushed along the sea floor by waves and on balance are driven to the top of the beach where they collect as a steep ridge or bank known as a storm beach. The permeability of these cliff-foot pebble banks inhibits the power of the backwash to drag the sediments back seawards.

Longshore drift

In Bideford Bay the most frequent waves are from the open Atlantic and have a westerly component. The waves tend to strike the storm beach obliquely pushing the pebbles at the foot of the cliffs towards the east. The pebbles of the storm beach can be regarded as being on a giant conveyor belt which moves them alongshore until they eventually become part of Westward Ho! pebble ridge.

Whenever there is a cliff failure, the resulting apron of debris on the beach will eventually be moved by the waves, the disintegrated mudstones (muds) in suspension and the rounded sandstone blocks (pebbles) by longshore drift. Once this has been achieved the waves can resume their attack on the cliff which again begins to retreat.

At first, when the shore platform was narrow, the waves struck the cliffs directly from deep water so were at full power. The cliffs were cut quickly and were steep with little time for a weathered vegetated gentler slope to develop before it was undercut again.

As the shore platform widened so some of the power of the waves was lost in the turbulence as the waves crossed the shallow rock platform. As a result the cliffs were eroded more slowly and had time to weather into a gentler and vegetated slope. The profile on page 39 summarises this sequence.

If it is high tide and waves are breaking on the storm beach below, listen to the sea breathing - the deep crackling roar of the swash as a wave sweeps pebbles up the beach, followed by the weaker, higher-pitched sucking drag of the backwash. That is the sound of 'attrition' as pebbles round and polish one another in the rock-mill of the storm beach. The pebbles are also continually chipping and rubbing at the solid rock (abrasion) both at the foot of the cliff and where pebbles tumble along the rocky shore platform. The photo taken on the shore, below viewpoint E, illustrates this process.

As a fresh young geography teacher walking this coast with my father, I was anxious to expound my newly acquired interpretative skills. "Notice," I said, "how the lower part of this small sandstone stack has become polished by the passage of pebbles. Soon, blocks will be torn off to become pebbles in their own right. The leaning stack has also reached the point of imminent collapse."

"How soon?" asked my wise father. That was in 1960 as was the photo.

This year (2004), I returned to the same spot. The human ravages of time are all too apparent but it took me a long time to identify even the smallest of changes to the rock. Had I miscalculated?

First, and perhaps obviously, it is a reminder that 'soon' on a human timescale is different from 'soon' on any of the other timescales we have considered.

Secondly, even when physical processes modifying the landscape are understood, the rate of change is difficult to predict. Commonly in the physical landscape, dramatic changes, such as landslips or cliff failures, occur during high-intensity but statistically low-frequency events, such as a violent storm or floods. This may or may not be followed by a long period of relative inactivity.

One day, someone will walk this shore, perhaps even with this booklet in hand, and find that, overnight, this small stack has disappeared. It could be you!

41

Abbotsham Cliff lies immediately beyond Cornborough. Here as elsewhere the storm-beach of grey polished pebbles abuts the cliff-foot. This pebble bank is continuous from Clovelly to Westward Ho! Individual pebbles, rolled by the waves move in a slow procession eastwards along the beach face until, eventually they become part of the famous Westward Ho! pebble ridge.

The occasional red pebble, born of cliff falls from the red sandstone outcrop at Peppercombe, are comparative newcomers, having only joined the march some 2.5 miles (4 km) up the coast to the south-west.

Near vertical, unvegetated cliffs imply active undercutting by powerful waves but the gentle vegetated cliff in Paul Lewin's painting suggests that here at least, waves are relatively weak and that the cliff-line is only retreating slowly.

The reason for this is that seawards of Abbotsham Cliff the shore platform is exceptionally wide and so at high tide much of the energy of waves has already been lost as the breakers roll in across the rocky foreshore (see page 39).

E

Where will you walk now?

To complete the recommended circuit, return along the old railway track to the Mermaid's Pool viewpoint, then branch left to follow the coastal path across Seafield. The commentary continues below.

Other Options

Another option is to walk back to Westward Ho! from Cornborough along the pebbles at the foot of the cliff but only attempt this on a falling tide. Critical safety and tide information is to be found on the inside front cover. You also need to be nimble and have good balance, for walking along the pebbles is tiring and these pebbles tend to roll unexpectedly. If you attempt this walk you can pick up the commentary again at Mermaid's Pool, on the next page, although your perspective from below the cliffs will, of course, be different.

Alternatively, before walking back, you may simply wish to extend your walk to include the shore at Cornborough or Abbotsham Cliff or the lime kiln at Green Cliff. All can be reached by continuing along the waymarked coastal footpath.

Keeping an eye on the vegetation

As you walk back notice the way that the vegetation reflects the cliff-top location, as suggested on page 34. On this first stretch the effect of exposure to wind and salt spray is marked. In the more sheltered hollows, where soil has accumulated, the climax vegetation is a stunted woodland, still severely pruned by the salt-laden storms. Here you may find sallow, blackthorn and ferns. On these trees lichens flourish in the damp, clean Atlantic air.

After passing the Mermaid's Pool viewpoint, the coast swings east. Look at the woodland on the more sheltered north-facing slopes of Kipling Tors. The trees are still wind-pruned but with less salt and some shelter, they can grow to a greater height, particularly in the small valleys and more sheltered areas. More exposed areas are covered in bracken, bramble, gorse and spring flowers such as celandine, bluebell and foxglove. Foxgloves, gorse and bracken are typical plants of these acid soils.

43

Mermaid's Pool Overlook revisited

At high tide the sandstone rocks on the immediate seaward side of Mermaid's Pool form an island stack. The stack offers a fascinating little timescale puzzle which I am reminded of each time I stop at this viewpoint.

Some years ago, standing here looking down on Mermaid's Pool at low tide (photograph on page 29), I noted that, spread across the dark mudstone platform were a number of boulders of pale sandstone, all grouped on the north-east side of the stack.

It was clear that these were blocks of sandstone which had become detached from the stack, probably during violent storms when powerful Atlantic breakers smash over the stack from the west and would push any detached blocks east.

I took my first photo from here in 1960 and, as a frequent visitor, decided to shoot a sequence of photos over the years. From these could be calculated the rate of boulder movement and the arrival of new boulders broken from the stack. This could then perhaps be linked to high intensity, exceptional storm events.

As the years passed, the photos and detailed mapping established that, in fact, no longshore movement of any of the plotted boulders was taking place and no new blocks were being added to the collection.

This was not at all what I was expecting. It implies that there have been no storms since 1960 which have been powerful enough to detach blocks from the stack or move any of the mapped boulders eastwards.

It would be interesting to extend the timescale by examining any photos taken of Mermaid's Pool between 1860 and 1960. Might somebody living locally be able to help? Eventually visual evidence might emerge for a 'mother of all storms'!

Similarly, one day, someone will look down on Mermaid's Pool and notice that the boulders have moved! How soon is soon?

One complication is that the displaced boulders have now been static for so long that a natural cement has bonded the boulders to the shore platform, making it even more difficult for them to be dislodged by storms.

Seafield Cliff

Walking to Viewpoint F

From the Mermaid's Pool Overlook, start walking back towards Westward Ho! but then almost immediately swing left leaving the old railway track to cut across the grassy field known as Seafield. After some 50 metres, where the rough path passes near the cliff, pause. We will call this viewpoint F. Beware of the unstable cliff edge.

Anticipating the unseen

'Reading the landscape' includes being able to imagine the unseen. What lies concealed beneath your feet? First, on the photo roughly locate your position. The gentle green slope is Seafield.

Turn to face the Tors. These were the sea-cliffs on which you were standing, 125,000 years ago, at the beginning of the walk (page 20). Kipling Tors may look a bit far inland for the sea to have eroded 70-metre high cliffs but don't forget that at that time sea-level was eight metres higher than that of the present day.

At the foot of this ancient cliff was a rocky shore platform, fashioned in much the same way as the modern intertidal platform but cut into the cliffs at about eight metres above the present shore. At the foot of the ancient cliff was a pebble storm beach resting on that old platform.

All is revealed?

All this would remain concealed beneath your feet but for the fact that modern waves have eroded a new cliff which, with exceptional clarity, has exposed the features of the old shoreline in the new cliff-face.

Looking along the shore, without approaching too close to the cliff edge, or by using the photographs, perhaps you can identify the features of this otherwise hidden 'fossil' landscape. The numbered landscape is revealed in more detail overleaf.

45

Putting things in order

By pulling together the strands of evidence provided by this view, a chronological reconstruction of the landscape evolution of this coast can be made.

125,000 years ago

In the last warm interglacial stage the sea carved cliffs at Kipling Tors (7) at the same time cutting an inter-tidal shore platform (4), the surface of which can be seen halfway up the modern sea-cliff. This marks the high sea-level of that time. At the base of the Kipling Tors cliff and sitting on the 8 m shore platform was a storm beach of pebbles (5) again today exposed in the cliff-face and called a raised beach. By about 100,000 years ago falling temperatures plunged Britain into an ice age and sea-levels fell, abandoning the old cliff line and beach.

18,000 years ago

The coldest trough within the last ice age was only some 18,000 years ago. By this time, the cliffs of Kipling Tors had been reduced to a frost-shattered slope looking very similar to the slope we see today. The frost debris, 'head', oozed down the slope each summer to collect at the foot of the tors as a thick layer of angular fragments (6) which buried the raised beach (5).

6,000 years ago to today

By 6,000 years ago the present warm interglacial was well underway and sea-level was close to today's. A new shore platform was being, and continues to be, created (1) as new cliffs (3) are cut into the old shore platform, raised beach and cap of 'head'. Present high tide is marked by another pebble storm beach (2) and continues to be fed by falling cliff debris and moves along shore by longshore drift.

46

Major elements of the history and landscape evolution of even a small area such as this must remain speculative and dependant upon knowledge brought to the scene. Yet the landscape itself provides so many visual clues about its past that a reasonably clear picture of the evolution of a landscape can often be put together by careful observation and interpretation. The closer you look the more detail is revealed and the more intriguing little stories emerge.

Raised beach overwhelmed

For example, as one might expect, the pebbles of the raised beach are identical in composition to the sandstone pebbles of the present storm beach. Yet, on inspection, unlike the modern beach, they seem to 'float' in a matrix of finer, fragments. Also some pebbles are broken but the shattered fragments remain undisturbed. What has happened here?

During the tundra conditions of the last ice age, the pebble beach was overwhelmed by the down-slope movement of soggy frost-shattered material (head). The resulting

jumbled mass, including the pebbles, was moved further downslope before being deposited at its present site. Later, presumably after slope movement had stopped, some pebbles fractured in the intense cold as water trapped in cracked pebbles froze.

A pebble-scalloped form

A little further east along the raised beach another small fragment of history reveals itself. Here, on the face of the fossil shore platform, perched well above the present beach, is a curved polished sculptured form.

This surely must be a feature worn by the passage of pebbles along a high-level beach some 125,000 years ago, much as the pebbles are polishing the rocks today (page 41).

The thrill of recognising the story told by these seemingly mundane small features, particularly when discovered for the first time, is not something that can be measured in scientific relevance but is more to do with recapturing a lost sense of (childhood?) wonder and an appreciation of the layers of time both human and physical which have contributed to the story of this place.

You are now in sight of the car park at Seafield and the end of this walk.

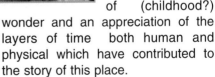

Acknowledgments

As an educational charity dedicated to encouraging the interpretation and appreciation of valued environments, Thematic Trails depends on the freely given time and expertise of a host of individuals. We particularly thank the following individuals for their help during the preparation of this book: Chris Cornford and Pip Jollands of the Hallsannery Field Centre, Bideford; Janet Keene of Thematic Trails and Susan Brown and Christopher Green of the Geologists' Association.

For the use of illustrative material we thank: Paul Lewin of Rose Cottage, Abbotsham, for permission to reproduce paintings of: 'Cornborough Cliffs, summer morning' (front cover), 'Cornborough Cliffs' (page 37) and 'Abbotsham Cliff, early light' (page 42). The air photographs of the Cornborough shore on pages 38 and 42 are by Roger Chope of Abbotsham Court. The paintings of 'Bideford Bay' on page 26 and 'Storm Reef' on this page are by my late father, Jo Keene, who loved this coast. The photograph of the bone harpoon on page 14 was provided by the 'Museum of Barnstaple and North Devon'. The watercolour 'Estuary of the River Taw, Devon' by Thomas Girtin (page 6) is reproduced by kind permission of the Yale Center for British Art, New Haven, USA, in association with The Bridgeman Art Library, 17-19 Garway Road, London W2 4PH

ENGLISH
NATURE

Publication of this book was assisted by the generous support of English Nature and the Geologists' Association Curry Fund